HOW SMARTPHONES ARE REWIRING OUR MINDS

Why Your Pocket Device Might Be Shrinking Your Brain and What You Can Do About It

Alejandro S. Diego

Table of Contents

INTRODUCTION..3

CHAPTER 1: THE RISE OF SMARTPHONES............. 7

CHAPTER 2: THE BRAIN'S RESPONSE TO SMARTPHONES..16

CHAPTER 3: MEMORY AND COGNITIVE DECLINE.25

CHAPTER 4: THE SILENT EPIDEMIC OF SMARTPHONE ADDICTION....................................... 35

CHAPTER 5: THE COGNITIVE FUNCTION CRISIS.. 45

CHAPTER 6: STRESS AND THE BIOLOGICAL TOLL.. 57

CHAPTER 7: SOCIAL MEDIA'S ROLE IN MENTAL HEALTH.. 69

CHAPTER 8: THE PATH FORWARD - RECLAIMING YOUR MIND.. 81

CONCLUSION.. 93

INTRODUCTION

In 2040, the world is unrecognizable from what we once knew. The sky hums with the quiet whirr of drones, autonomous vehicles glide through streets once filled with human drivers, and virtual reality has become indistinguishable from the real world. But beneath the surface of these technological marvels lies a subtle, insidious transformation that has occurred within us—one that we might not fully grasp until it's too late.

As we march forward into this brave new world, smartphones—those ubiquitous little rectangles that have become an extension of our very selves—have subtly and steadily rewired our minds. These devices, once heralded as the pinnacle of human ingenuity, are now reshaping our brains in ways that few could have predicted. The changes are not just superficial; they go deep, altering how we think, how we remember, how we interact with the world around us.

It's not just about the technology we hold in our hands—it's about what it's doing to our very essence as human beings. The once clear lines between reality and the digital world have blurred, and with it, our cognitive functions have begun to shift. Memory, once a robust and vital part of our intelligence, is now outsourced to the devices we trust more than our own minds. Our ability to focus, to think deeply and critically, has been fractured by the constant barrage of notifications and the endless scroll of information. And as we become more dependent on these devices, the question that haunts us is whether we are the masters of our technology or its slaves.

But why should this matter to you? Because the stakes have never been higher. We stand at a crossroads, where the decisions we make today about how we use technology will determine the kind of world we live in tomorrow. It's not just about convenience or efficiency—it's about the survival of our cognitive autonomy, our ability to think independently, and our very humanity.

As we delve into this exploration, we will uncover the unseen costs of our reliance on smartphones. We will examine the scientific evidence that paints a concerning picture of our future and offer insights into how we can reclaim our minds in this age of digital distraction. This journey is not just an intellectual exercise—it is a call to action, a plea for us to wake up to the changes happening within us before it's too late.

In this book, you will discover not just the problems, but the solutions. You will learn how to navigate this technological landscape without losing yourself in the process. Because the future is not set in stone, and while technology will undoubtedly continue to evolve, so too can we. The choice is ours to make—will we let our minds be shaped by the devices in our pockets, or will we take back control and shape our own destiny?

Welcome to the future. The story of how smartphones are rewiring our minds begins now. And trust me, you'll want to keep reading. The implications are far greater than you might think.

CHAPTER 1: THE RISE OF SMARTPHONES

The launch of the first iPhone in 2007 marked a watershed moment in the history of technology, setting in motion a revolution that would transform the way we live, work, and interact with the world around us. Before the iPhone, mobile phones were primarily used for calls and texts, with a few offering rudimentary web browsing and basic games. The concept of a smartphone—a device that could seamlessly integrate multiple functionalities into one sleek, portable package—was still in its infancy.

When Steve Jobs took the stage on January 9, 2007, to unveil the iPhone, he introduced it as three devices in one: "a widescreen iPod with touch controls, a revolutionary mobile phone, and a breakthrough internet communications device." But it was more than just the sum of these parts. The iPhone's true innovation lay in its design and user interface. For the first time, a phone featured a large, multi-touch screen that eliminated the need for physical buttons, allowing users to interact with their devices in an entirely new way—through taps, swipes, and pinches.

This combination of intuitive design and powerful technology quickly captivated the public's imagination. Within months, the iPhone became a cultural phenomenon, heralding a new era of mobile computing. It was not just a phone; it was a status symbol, a gateway to the internet, and a personal assistant all in one. The iPhone's success was not just due to its hardware but also to its software ecosystem. The introduction of the App Store in 2008 revolutionized the way software was distributed and consumed, allowing developers to create a vast array of applications that extended the functionality of the iPhone far beyond its original capabilities.

As the iPhone evolved over the years, it continued to push the boundaries of what a smartphone could do. Each new iteration brought improvements in speed, camera quality, battery life, and design, but more importantly, it integrated new technologies that further blurred the lines between the physical and digital worlds. Features like GPS, accelerometers, and gyroscopes enabled a host of new applications, from navigation to fitness tracking, while the introduction of Siri, Apple's voice-activated assistant, brought a new level of interactivity and convenience to users.

The iPhone also played a pivotal role in the rise of social media, providing a platform for apps like Facebook, Instagram, and Twitter to flourish. With a camera always at hand, users could capture and share their lives in real-time, fueling the growth of a connected, always-on culture that has come to define the modern era.

Beyond its technological innovations, the iPhone also had a profound impact on the global economy.

It spurred the growth of the smartphone industry, leading to intense competition and rapid innovation as companies like Samsung, Google, and Huawei raced to develop their own devices to rival the iPhone. The iPhone also transformed industries such as telecommunications, entertainment, and retail, as businesses adapted to the new mobile-first world.

Looking back, it's clear that the launch of the iPhone in 2007 was not just the beginning of a new product line for Apple; it was the beginning of a new era. The iPhone changed the way we communicate, the way we access information, and the way we live our daily lives. It set the stage for the smartphone to become an indispensable tool in the 21st century, a device that has fundamentally reshaped our world in ways that are still unfolding today.

As we reflect on the birth of the iPhone, we can see that its impact goes far beyond the realm of technology. It has altered our social fabric, influenced global economies, and even reshaped our brains, as we will explore further in the pages to come. The iPhone is not just a piece of hardware; it is a symbol of the profound changes that have come to define our modern age.

When the first iPhone was released in 2007, it was met with widespread excitement and anticipation. The idea of having a powerful, pocket-sized computer that could make calls, send texts, play music, and browse the internet was revolutionary. Early reactions to the iPhone and other emerging smartphones were overwhelmingly positive, as people quickly embraced the convenience and connectivity these devices offered. The ability to access information at any time, stay in constant communication with others, and carry a virtual library of apps in your pocket felt like a glimpse into the future—a future that was now within reach.

The perceived benefits of smartphones were immediately apparent. They offered a level of convenience that had never been seen before. Tasks that once required multiple devices—a phone, a computer, a camera, a GPS—could now be done with a single device that fit comfortably in your hand. For many, smartphones represented a significant leap forward in personal productivity. The ability to check emails, manage calendars, and stay organized while on the go made smartphones an indispensable tool for both work and personal life. Social media platforms also flourished, as smartphones made it easier than ever to stay connected with friends and family, share experiences, and engage with the world in real-time.

However, as the excitement of these early years began to settle, unforeseen consequences started to emerge. The very features that made smartphones so appealing—constant connectivity, instant access to information, and an endless stream of entertainment—began to reveal their darker sides. What initially seemed like a leap forward in convenience and productivity started to show signs of overuse and dependence.

One of the first signs of trouble was the growing sense of distraction that smartphones brought into daily life. The constant barrage of notifications, alerts, and messages made it difficult to focus on any one task for an extended period. This "always-on" culture, while beneficial in some respects, began to take a toll on people's ability to concentrate and engage deeply with their surroundings. What was once hailed as a tool for productivity started to become a source of constant interruption, leading to a decline in the quality of both work and personal interactions.

Moreover, as smartphones became more integrated into daily life, their impact on mental health and well-being became more apparent. The relentless pressure to stay connected and keep up with the fast-paced digital world began to contribute to rising levels of stress and anxiety. Social media, in particular, played a significant role in this, as people found themselves constantly comparing their lives to the curated highlights of others, leading to feelings of inadequacy and dissatisfaction.

As time went on, it became clear that the impact of smartphones extended far beyond mere distraction. Studies began to show that prolonged smartphone use could have more profound effects on cognitive function, memory, and even brain structure. The constant reliance on smartphones for tasks like navigation, information retrieval, and communication was shown to reduce our mental agility and weaken our ability to recall information. The once-unthinkable idea that a device meant to make us smarter and more efficient could actually be diminishing our cognitive capabilities started to gain traction.

The long-term effects that were not anticipated at the time of the smartphone's introduction now form a complex web of consequences that we are only beginning to fully understand. What started as a tool for connection and convenience has evolved into a device that, while still immensely useful, also poses significant challenges to our mental and emotional well-being. The very nature of how we think, interact, and perceive the world has been subtly but significantly altered by the smartphones that have become so deeply woven into the fabric of modern life.

As we continue to explore the role of smartphones in our lives, it is essential to recognize both their benefits and their drawbacks. The early excitement surrounding these devices was not misplaced, but neither were the concerns that have since arisen. Understanding these unforeseen consequences is crucial as we navigate the increasingly complex relationship between technology and humanity.

CHAPTER 2: THE BRAIN'S RESPONSE TO SMARTPHONES

As you hold your smartphone in your hand, scrolling through social media, checking notifications, or playing a game, you might not realize that your brain is engaged in a complex dance of chemicals, particularly one called dopamine. This neurotransmitter, often referred to as the "feel-good" chemical, plays a crucial role in how we experience pleasure, motivation, and reward. The creators of smartphones and the apps that run on them have cleverly designed these devices to tap into this natural dopamine system, creating feedback loops that keep us coming back for more.

Dopamine is released in the brain when we experience something pleasurable, whether it's eating delicious food, receiving a compliment, or achieving a goal. It's the brain's way of reinforcing behaviors that are beneficial for survival and well-being. However, in the context of smartphone use, this system can be hijacked in ways that may not always serve our best interests.

Every time you receive a notification, like a post, or even anticipate a new message, your brain experiences a small surge of dopamine. This release creates a feeling of satisfaction and encourages you to repeat the action that triggered it. Over time, this can create a powerful feedback loop: you check your phone, you get a hit of dopamine, and you feel good, so you check your phone again. The more this cycle repeats, the more ingrained the behavior becomes, often leading to habitual or even compulsive smartphone use.

The designers of apps and smartphone interfaces understand this process intimately. They have crafted their products to maximize these dopamine loops, ensuring that users remain engaged for as long as possible. Features like "likes" on social media, notifications, and the endless scroll are not just convenient—they are intentionally designed to keep you hooked. Each interaction is a small, gratifying reward that makes you want to continue using the app, creating a cycle that can be hard to break.

This exploitation of our brain's reward system is particularly evident in social media platforms. When you post a photo or share an update, the anticipation of receiving likes, comments, and shares triggers a dopamine release even before the feedback comes in. Once the notifications start rolling in, each one reinforces the behavior, making you more likely to post again and again. This creates a kind of dependency, where your brain begins to crave the next hit of social approval, just like a gambler craves the next big win.

But the effects of these dopamine loops extend beyond mere habit formation. Over time, constant exposure to these quick hits of pleasure can lead to desensitization. Just as with any other form of stimulation, the more frequently you experience a dopamine surge, the more you need to achieve the same level of satisfaction. This can result in a need to check your phone more often, spend more time on apps, or seek out more intense forms of engagement to achieve the same sense of reward.

In some cases, this can lead to what experts refer to as "dopamine burnout." The constant chase for that next reward can overwhelm the brain's dopamine system, making it harder to experience pleasure from everyday activities that once brought joy. This is why some people report feeling restless, anxious, or dissatisfied when they're not engaging with their phones—over time, the brain has become conditioned to seek out the quick, easy rewards that smartphones provide, leaving other activities feeling dull by comparison.

The design of smartphones and their apps is a testament to the power of understanding human psychology. By tapping into our natural tendencies for feedback and reward, these devices have become deeply integrated into our lives, often in ways that we might not fully realize or control. The challenge, then, is to become aware of these loops and find ways to break free from their hold. By understanding how smartphones exploit our dopamine system, we can begin to take steps to regain control over our attention and our lives.

The addictive nature of smartphones is no accident. It's the result of a careful and deliberate understanding of human psychology, particularly the mechanisms that drive habit formation and addiction. At the core of this is dopamine, the brain's primary reward neurotransmitter. But addiction to smartphones goes beyond just chemical responses; it also involves the way these devices are designed, especially the algorithms that power the apps we use daily. Together, these elements create a potent mix that can keep us glued to our screens, sometimes at the expense of our mental health.

Dopamine plays a crucial role in the development of addiction. When we engage in activities that are rewarding—whether it's eating our favorite food, winning a game, or receiving praise—dopamine is released in the brain. This creates a sense of pleasure and reinforces the behavior, making us more likely to repeat it in the future. In the context of smartphone use, each time we receive a notification, check a message, or see a "like" on social media, our brain releases a small burst of dopamine. This release is what makes these actions feel good and why we are so inclined to repeat them, sometimes compulsively.

However, the addictive potential of smartphones is not just about the dopamine rush from individual interactions; it's also about the unpredictability of these rewards. Psychologists have long known that variable rewards—rewards that are not guaranteed but come at random intervals—are particularly powerful in creating addictive behaviors. This is the principle behind gambling, where the uncertainty of winning makes the act of playing more compelling. Similarly, with smartphones, the unpredictability of notifications, the chance that a message might contain something important or exciting, and the random rewards from apps all contribute to making smartphone use highly addictive.

But dopamine is only one piece of the puzzle. The algorithms that drive the apps on our smartphones are designed to exploit this natural inclination towards addictive behavior. These algorithms are crafted to keep us engaged for as long as possible, often by feeding us content that is most likely to hold our attention. Social media platforms, in particular, use sophisticated algorithms to analyze our behavior—what we like, share, comment on, and how long we spend on different types of content. This data is then used to tailor our feeds, ensuring that we see more of what keeps us engaged and, consequently, more time spent on the platform.

These algorithms are not benign. They are designed with one primary goal in mind: to maximize user engagement. This means showing you content that is emotionally charged, whether it's something that makes you happy, angry, or outraged. Emotionally charged content tends to generate more interaction, which in turn, triggers more dopamine release. This creates a feedback loop where the more you engage, the more the algorithm learns about what keeps you engaged, and the more it feeds you similar content.

This cycle can have significant consequences for mental health. The constant exposure to emotionally charged content can lead to heightened levels of stress, anxiety, and even depression. Social media, with its curated images and highlight reels, can also contribute to feelings of inadequacy or FOMO (fear of missing out), as users compare their lives to the seemingly perfect lives of others. The algorithms don't just keep us engaged; they often do so by amplifying negative emotions, which can have a lasting impact on our well-being.

Moreover, the design of these apps often includes features that make it difficult to disengage. Infinite scrolling, autoplay videos, and push notifications are all engineered to keep you on your device longer than you might have intended. The goal is not just to capture your attention but to hold it, sometimes for hours on end, leading to a cycle of usage that can feel impossible to break.

Understanding the science behind smartphone addiction, from the role of dopamine to the influence of algorithms, is crucial in recognizing the challenges we face in managing our screen time. These devices, designed to be indispensable tools, have the potential to shape our behaviors in ways that are not always in our best interest. As we become more aware of these mechanisms, we can begin to take steps to mitigate their impact, reclaiming our time and attention from the grip of these digital addictions.

CHAPTER 3: MEMORY AND COGNITIVE DECLINE

In a world where our smartphones have become extensions of ourselves, the once vital mental skill of memory has quietly begun to atrophy. This phenomenon, often referred to as the "memory muscle," describes the brain's ability to remember and process information—a skill that, like any muscle, requires regular exercise to remain strong. However, as we increasingly rely on our smartphones to store information, navigate our surroundings, and manage our lives, this memory muscle is getting less and less of a workout.

Before the advent of smartphones, people had to rely heavily on their memories to manage daily life. Whether it was remembering phone numbers, appointments, or directions, our brains were constantly engaged in storing and recalling information. This regular mental exercise kept the hippocampus, the area of the brain responsible for memory formation, active and robust. However, with the rise of smartphones, much of this cognitive workload has been offloaded to our devices.

Take, for example, the simple task of remembering a phone number. In the past, you might have memorized the numbers of your closest friends and family members. Today, with a few taps on a screen, you can instantly access a contact list that stores hundreds of numbers. While this is undoubtedly convenient, it also means that your brain is no longer required to remember these details, leading to a gradual weakening of the neural pathways associated with memory.

This reliance on smartphones extends to other areas as well. GPS applications have all but eliminated the need to remember directions or navigate using landmarks. Calendars and reminders on our phones ensure that we don't have to remember appointments or deadlines. Even the simplest of facts, once committed to memory, can now be quickly Googled, reducing the need for internal retention of information.

The consequence of this shift is not merely that we remember less, but that our brains are adapting to this new reality by prioritizing other cognitive functions over memory. This phenomenon, known as "cognitive offloading," allows the brain to conserve energy and resources by outsourcing certain tasks to external tools. While this can free up mental capacity for other activities, it also means that the neural networks involved in memory are being used less frequently, leading to their gradual weakening.

Research has shown that this decline in memory function is not just theoretical. Studies have found that people who rely heavily on their smartphones for information recall have lower levels of activity in the hippocampus. Over time, this reduced activity can lead to a decrease in the size and efficiency of the hippocampus, making it harder to form and retain new memories.

Moreover, this weakening of the memory muscle can have broader implications for cognitive health. The hippocampus is also involved in other critical functions, such as spatial navigation and emotional regulation. As its activity diminishes, these areas of cognitive function can also be affected. In extreme cases, prolonged inactivity in the hippocampus has been linked to an increased risk of cognitive decline and conditions such as dementia.

However, the impact of smartphones on memory is not just about the loss of mental exercise. The constant presence of a device that can instantly retrieve any piece of information changes the way we process and store memories. Instead of deeply encoding information into long-term memory, we may only partially process it, relying on the knowledge that it can be easily retrieved later. This superficial processing leads to weaker, more fragile memories that are easily forgotten.

As our memory muscle continues to weaken, it is essential to recognize the importance of exercising it regularly. Just as physical muscles require regular use to stay strong, so too does our memory. Simple practices, such as trying to remember phone numbers, directions, or even the details of a conversation without relying on a smartphone, can help keep the hippocampus active and engaged.

In a world where our devices do so much for us, it's easy to let our natural cognitive abilities atrophy. But by consciously choosing to challenge our memory, we can keep this vital mental muscle strong and healthy, ensuring that we retain the ability to remember and process information long after the novelty of our smartphones has worn off.

Scientific research has increasingly focused on understanding the effects of smartphone use on the brain, particularly concerning the hippocampus, the region responsible for memory formation and spatial navigation. Several studies have revealed troubling findings that suggest excessive smartphone use can lead to a reduction in the size of the hippocampus and a decrease in gray matter volume in critical areas of the brain.

One notable study conducted in 2021 examined the brains of individuals who reported heavy smartphone use. Using MRI scans, researchers discovered that these individuals had a significantly smaller hippocampus compared to those who used their smartphones less frequently. The reduction in hippocampal size was particularly evident in younger participants, whose brains are still developing, raising concerns about the long-term effects of smartphone reliance on cognitive health.

Another meta-analysis of multiple studies reinforced these findings, revealing that chronic smartphone use is associated with lower gray matter volumes in several key brain regions, including the anterior cingulate cortex, orbitofrontal cortex, fusiform gyrus, and parahippocampal areas. Gray matter is crucial for processing information, making decisions, and regulating emotions, and its reduction can have widespread effects on overall cognitive function.

These findings are not just theoretical but have real-world implications that many people experience daily. One of the most common manifestations of this cognitive decline is the growing dependency on GPS for navigation. In the past, people relied on memory and spatial reasoning to find their way around, often recalling routes and landmarks. Today, however, many individuals rely almost exclusively on GPS, allowing the device to dictate their movements. This reliance on external tools can weaken the brain's natural ability to form and retain spatial memories, leading to a reduction in hippocampal activity.

The consequences of this dependency extend beyond navigation. Forgetting important information, such as appointments, deadlines, or even the details of a conversation, has become increasingly common. As people rely more on their smartphones to store and recall information, their brains engage less in the process of deeply encoding memories. This leads to weaker, less durable memories that are easily forgotten, contributing to a cycle of increased reliance on smartphones for even the simplest tasks.

Recognizing these challenges is the first step in mitigating their impact. Fortunately, there are practical strategies that can help strengthen memory and reduce smartphone dependence. One of the most effective approaches is to engage in regular mental exercises that challenge the brain to remember and process information without the aid of a smartphone. For example, trying to navigate familiar routes without GPS, memorizing phone numbers, or recalling the details of a conversation can all help keep the hippocampus active and engaged.

Another important strategy is to set boundaries around smartphone use. Limiting the time spent on devices, particularly during activities that require focus and memory, can help reduce cognitive offloading. Simple practices like turning off notifications, designating "phone-free" times, or even using a physical planner instead of a digital one can encourage the brain to take on more of the cognitive load, strengthening memory over time.

Mindfulness and meditation are also powerful tools for improving memory and cognitive function. These practices help increase focus and awareness, allowing the brain to process and store information more effectively. Studies have shown that regular meditation can actually increase gray matter in the hippocampus, counteracting some of the negative effects of smartphone use.

Incorporating physical exercise into daily routines is another way to support brain health. Exercise has been shown to increase blood flow to the brain, promote the growth of new neurons, and improve overall cognitive function. Activities like walking, swimming, or even yoga can help keep the brain and body in optimal condition.

As we navigate the challenges of living in a digital age, it's essential to find a balance between the convenience of technology and the preservation of our cognitive abilities. By taking proactive steps to engage our memory muscles and reduce our reliance on smartphones, we can protect our brains from the potential negative effects of modern technology and ensure that we maintain our cognitive health for years to come.

CHAPTER 4: THE SILENT EPIDEMIC OF SMARTPHONE ADDICTION

In today's hyperconnected world, where smartphones have become an integral part of our daily lives, a new phenomenon has emerged: nomophobia, or the fear of being without your phone. The term "nomophobia" is short for "no mobile phone phobia," and it encapsulates the anxiety and discomfort that many people feel when they are disconnected from their smartphones. This fear is not just a passing concern but a deep-seated anxiety that can have significant implications for mental health and overall well-being.

Nomophobia stems from the increasing reliance on smartphones for a wide range of activities, from communication and navigation to entertainment and information gathering. For many, the thought of being without their phone is unsettling because it represents a loss of control, connection, and security. Smartphones have become our lifelines, linking us to the world around us, and the idea of losing that connection can trigger intense feelings of vulnerability and fear.

The implications of nomophobia are far-reaching. On a psychological level, the constant need to be near one's phone can lead to heightened levels of stress and anxiety. People with nomophobia may experience panic or discomfort when they are unable to check their phones, even for short periods. This can manifest in various ways, such as constantly checking for notifications, feeling uneasy when the phone's battery is low, or avoiding situations where phone use is restricted.

Moreover, nomophobia can have a profound impact on daily life. It can interfere with personal relationships, as the need to stay connected to the phone can detract from face-to-face interactions. For example, someone with nomophobia might struggle to fully engage in conversations or social activities, constantly distracted by the urge to check their phone. This can lead to a sense of isolation, even when surrounded by others, as the smartphone becomes a barrier rather than a bridge to meaningful connection.

The fear of being without a phone can also affect productivity and concentration. In professional settings, nomophobia can lead to a lack of focus, as individuals may find it difficult to concentrate on tasks without the reassurance of their phone nearby. This constant distraction can reduce efficiency, hinder problem-solving abilities, and contribute to a general sense of overwhelm.

In more severe cases, nomophobia can exacerbate other mental health issues, such as anxiety disorders or depression. The constant need for validation and reassurance from social media or communication apps can create a cycle of dependence, where individuals rely on their phones to manage their emotions. This can lead to a decline in mental health, as the phone becomes a crutch rather than a tool for enhancing well-being.

Addressing nomophobia requires a conscious effort to understand and manage one's relationship with technology. It involves recognizing the signs of smartphone dependency and taking steps to reduce the reliance on constant connectivity. For some, this might mean setting boundaries around phone use, such as designated "phone-free" times during the day or creating physical spaces where phones are not allowed. For others, it might involve exploring alternative ways to manage anxiety, such as through mindfulness practices or seeking support from mental health professionals.

Ultimately, overcoming nomophobia is about reclaiming control over one's life and recognizing that true connection and security come from within, not from a device. By learning to live without the constant need for our phones, we can begin to break free from the anxiety that they can create and find a healthier, more balanced approach to technology in our lives.

Smartphones, though designed to be tools of convenience, have evolved into powerful devices that can foster addictive behaviors similar to those seen in casinos. The parallels between smartphone usage and gambling addiction are striking, particularly in how both environments exploit psychological vulnerabilities to keep users engaged. Understanding these techniques and their psychological impact is crucial for anyone looking to regain control over their smartphone use.

One of the most potent techniques employed by both casinos and smartphones is the use of variable rewards. In a casino, the unpredictability of winning on a slot machine—sometimes hitting the jackpot, other times winning nothing—keeps players coming back for more. This randomness creates a sense of anticipation and excitement that is highly addictive. Similarly, smartphones are designed to deliver unpredictable rewards, whether it's a new like on a social media post, a message notification, or an update in a game. This uncertainty, combined with the possibility of a rewarding experience, keeps users compulsively checking their devices.

Another common technique is the use of "pull-to-refresh" and infinite scrolling. These features mimic the action of pulling the lever on a slot machine, where each pull offers the chance of a reward. On social media or news apps, pulling down to refresh the feed or endlessly scrolling through content creates a continuous loop of anticipation and gratification. This design keeps users engaged for extended periods, often far longer than they intended.

The impact of these addictive behaviors on mental health can be profound. As users become more accustomed to the frequent dopamine hits from smartphone interactions, their brains start to crave these rewards more intensely. Over time, this can lead to a form of dependency where individuals feel compelled to check their phones even when it's not necessary. The constant need for validation through likes, comments, and messages can create anxiety, particularly when these rewards are not forthcoming.

Withdrawal symptoms are another significant consequence of smartphone addiction. Just as with substance addiction, users may experience feelings of irritability, restlessness, or even panic when they are unable to access their phones. This withdrawal can occur in situations where phone use is restricted, such as during meetings, flights, or social gatherings. The discomfort felt during these times can further reinforce the dependency, as individuals may seek to avoid such situations in the future.

The continuous use of smartphones also contributes to a decrease in attention span. The constant barrage of notifications and the temptation to multitask between apps and activities can make it difficult for users to focus on a single task for an extended period. This fragmented attention not only reduces productivity but also impairs the ability to engage in deep, meaningful thought or conversations. The result is a society where individuals are increasingly distracted, less able to concentrate, and more prone to stress.

Breaking the cycle of smartphone addiction requires a proactive approach and a willingness to make changes in daily habits. One of the most effective strategies is to use digital wellbeing features that many smartphones now offer. These tools are designed to help users monitor and manage their screen time, providing insights into how much time is spent on various apps and allowing users to set limits on usage. For example, setting a daily screen time limit or scheduling "downtime" periods where only essential apps are accessible can help reduce the compulsion to check the phone constantly.

Another useful technique is to create physical boundaries around smartphone use. This might involve designating certain areas of the home, such as the bedroom or dining room, as phone-free zones, or setting specific times of day when the phone is put away. These boundaries can help reduce the temptation to use the phone mindlessly and encourage more intentional, focused interactions.

Mindfulness practices can also play a crucial role in breaking smartphone addiction. Techniques such as meditation, deep breathing, and mindfulness exercises can help individuals become more aware of their phone use and the triggers that lead to compulsive checking. By developing greater self-awareness, users can begin to recognize when they are reaching for their phone out of habit rather than necessity and make more conscious decisions about when and how to use it.

Finally, seeking support from others can be invaluable in managing smartphone addiction. Whether through a support group, counseling, or simply discussing the issue with friends and family, having a network of people who understand the challenges and can offer encouragement can make a significant difference.

In a world where smartphones are deeply integrated into daily life, managing their use can be challenging, but it is not impossible. By understanding the techniques that make these devices so addictive and employing strategies to reduce their grip, individuals can take back control and use their smartphones in a way that enhances, rather than detracts from, their lives.

CHAPTER 5: THE COGNITIVE FUNCTION CRISIS

In our increasingly connected world, smartphones have become so integral to our daily lives that many of us feel incomplete without them. But beyond their obvious utility, smartphones have a subtler, more insidious effect on our cognitive abilities—a phenomenon known as "brain drain." This concept refers to the cognitive overload that occurs simply from having a smartphone present, even if it's not in use. The mere proximity of a smartphone can drain our mental resources, leading to diminished cognitive performance and reduced ability to focus on tasks at hand.

The idea of brain drain is rooted in the understanding that our brains have a limited capacity to process information at any given time. When we attempt to focus on a task, whether it's solving a problem, engaging in a conversation, or absorbing new information, we need our full cognitive resources. However, when a smartphone is nearby, part of our attention is inevitably diverted, even if we aren't consciously aware of it. This division of attention leads to what's known as cognitive overload—a state where the brain is forced to juggle competing demands, resulting in reduced efficiency and effectiveness in performing tasks.

Studies have shown that simply having a smartphone within sight or within reach can impair cognitive performance. Researchers at the University of Chicago conducted experiments where participants were asked to complete a series of cognitive tasks. Some participants had their phones placed on the desk in front of them, while others were instructed to keep their phones out of sight, such as in a bag or another room. The results were striking: those with their phones visible performed significantly worse on the tasks than those whose phones were out of sight. This held true even though the phones were turned off or set to silent mode, indicating that the effect was not due to the distraction of notifications but to the mere presence of the device.

The brain drain effect occurs because the smartphone acts as a "constant competitor" for our attention. Even when we are not actively using it, our minds are subconsciously aware of the phone and the potential for it to interrupt us with a message, a call, or an update. This awareness creates a state of cognitive dissonance, where part of our mental energy is expended on resisting the urge to check the phone or simply thinking about it. As a result, our ability to concentrate fully on the task at hand is compromised.

This cognitive drain can have wide-reaching implications for various aspects of life. In academic settings, students who keep their phones nearby while studying or attending lectures may find it harder to retain information and perform well on exams. In the workplace, employees may struggle with productivity and creative problem-solving if their phones are within easy reach during meetings or while working on complex projects. Even in social interactions, the presence of a smartphone can hinder meaningful engagement, as individuals may find it difficult to fully listen and respond to others when part of their attention is diverted.

Moreover, the impact of brain drain extends beyond immediate cognitive performance. Over time, the constant cognitive load imposed by smartphones can lead to mental fatigue, stress, and burnout. The continuous need to manage multiple streams of information and the persistent tug-of-war between focusing on a task and the lure of the smartphone can exhaust our cognitive resources, leaving us less capable of deep thinking, creativity, and reflective thought.

To mitigate the effects of brain drain, it is essential to create environments that allow for uninterrupted focus and mental clarity. One effective strategy is to establish "phone-free" zones or times during the day when the smartphone is completely out of sight and out of reach. For example, keeping the phone in another room while working, studying, or engaging in social activities can help reduce the cognitive load and improve concentration.

Another approach is to practice digital mindfulness—becoming more aware of how and when we use our smartphones and making conscious decisions to limit their influence on our cognitive processes. This might involve setting specific times for checking emails and messages, rather than constantly being on alert for notifications, or using apps that promote focused work by temporarily disabling distractions.

In a world where smartphones are designed to be ever-present and always accessible, the concept of brain drain serves as a reminder of the importance of managing our relationship with technology. By understanding the cognitive costs of having a smartphone nearby and taking proactive steps to minimize its impact, we can reclaim our mental bandwidth and enhance our ability to think clearly, deeply, and effectively.

In the digital age, where screens dominate our lives, a growing body of research is revealing the subtle but significant differences between reading from a screen and reading from paper. These differences go beyond mere preference; they affect how we comprehend and retain information. When we read from a screen, whether it's a smartphone, tablet, or computer, our brains process the information differently than when we read from a physical book or printed material. This has profound implications for our ability to understand and remember what we read.

Studies have shown that reading from screens tends to be more superficial, with readers often skimming the text rather than engaging in deep, focused reading. The very design of screens, which encourages scrolling, clicking, and multitasking, can disrupt the linear flow of reading and make it harder to immerse oneself in the material. This skimming behavior leads to reduced comprehension, as readers are less likely to fully absorb and integrate the information. Additionally, the backlit nature of screens can cause eye strain and fatigue, further hindering the reading experience.

In contrast, reading from paper fosters a deeper engagement with the text. The tactile experience of holding a book and the absence of digital distractions allows readers to concentrate more fully on the material. Research has shown that when people read from paper, they are better able to understand complex ideas, retain information, and recall details later. The physical act of turning pages also helps with memory, as it creates a sense of location within the text—something that is often lost in the infinite scroll of digital screens.

The comprehension challenges associated with screen reading are further exacerbated by the widespread practice of multitasking. Smartphones, with their constant stream of notifications, messages, and updates, encourage us to divide our attention between multiple tasks. We might read an article, check a message, and scroll through social media all within the span of a few minutes. While this might feel productive, it actually comes at a significant cost to our cognitive function.

The myth of multitasking—the belief that we can effectively handle multiple tasks simultaneously—has been debunked by numerous studies. In reality, the human brain is not designed to multitask in the way that many of us attempt to do. Instead of processing tasks simultaneously, our brains rapidly switch between tasks, which diminishes our ability to focus on any one task deeply. This constant task-switching leads to shallow thinking, fragmented attention, and a reduction in the quality of our work.

When it comes to deep thinking and memory formation, multitasking is particularly detrimental. Deep thinking requires sustained attention and the ability to engage with complex ideas over an extended period. However, when our attention is constantly being pulled in different directions by our smartphones, we lose the capacity for deep, reflective thought. This not only impacts our ability to understand and analyze information but also weakens our memory. Without focused attention, information is less likely to be encoded into long-term memory, leading to forgetfulness and a shallow grasp of concepts.

Given these challenges, it's crucial to find ways to enhance cognitive function by reducing screen time and engaging in more mindful activities. One of the most effective strategies is to limit the time spent reading from screens and, when possible, opt for paper-based reading materials. Whether it's for studying, work, or leisure, reading from a physical book or printed article can improve comprehension and retention. Additionally, taking regular breaks from screens to rest the eyes and mind can help mitigate the negative effects of prolonged screen use.

Practicing mindfulness is another powerful tool for improving focus and cognitive function. Mindfulness involves being fully present in the moment and consciously directing one's attention to a single task. By practicing mindfulness, whether through meditation, focused breathing, or simply paying close attention to a specific activity, we can train our brains to resist the pull of distractions and engage more deeply with the task at hand.

Another way to enhance cognitive function is to establish boundaries around smartphone use. This might involve setting specific times of day when the phone is put away, turning off non-essential notifications, or creating designated "focus zones" where screens are not allowed. By creating an environment that minimizes distractions, we can improve our ability to concentrate, think deeply, and retain information.

Incorporating physical exercise into daily routines is also beneficial for cognitive health. Exercise has been shown to boost brain function, enhance memory, and improve overall mental clarity. Activities like walking, yoga, or even short bursts of physical activity throughout the day can help clear the mind and increase focus.

Lastly, fostering a habit of single-tasking—focusing on one task at a time rather than attempting to multitask—can significantly enhance cognitive function. By giving our full attention to a single activity, whether it's reading, working, or even having a conversation, we can improve our ability to think critically, solve problems, and form lasting memories.

In an age where screens and smartphones are omnipresent, it's essential to be mindful of how these tools impact our cognitive abilities. By making conscious choices to reduce screen time, engage in mindful activities, and focus our attention, we can protect and enhance our cognitive function, ensuring that we remain sharp, thoughtful, and capable in our digital world.

CHAPTER 6: STRESS AND THE BIOLOGICAL TOLL

In the age of constant connectivity, where our smartphones are rarely out of reach, the very devices designed to simplify our lives have become significant contributors to stress. The neuroscience behind this stress reveals how the barrage of notifications, messages, and alerts from our phones can trigger a cascade of reactions in the brain that heightens anxiety and disrupts our mental equilibrium.

At the heart of this stress response is the brain's limbic system, particularly the amygdala, which is responsible for processing emotions, including fear and anxiety. When a smartphone notification sounds, it can act as a modern-day alarm, triggering a surge of adrenaline and cortisol—hormones associated with the fight-or-flight response. This reaction might have served us well in a prehistoric environment, where immediate physical threats required quick action. However, in today's context, where the "threat" is often nothing more than a message or a social media update, this constant state of alertness can lead to chronic stress.

The brain's prefrontal cortex, which is involved in decision-making, problem-solving, and regulating emotions, also plays a crucial role in how we respond to smartphone-induced stress. When the prefrontal cortex is overwhelmed by constant notifications, its ability to regulate the amygdala's response is diminished. This imbalance leads to a heightened state of arousal, where even minor disruptions can cause significant stress. Over time, this can impair the brain's ability to manage stress effectively, leading to a cycle of anxiety and tension.

But the impact of smartphone-induced stress extends beyond the brain, affecting the entire body. Chronic stress, whether triggered by smartphone use or other factors, has well-documented physical health risks. Prolonged exposure to stress hormones like cortisol can lead to a range of health problems, including high blood pressure, weakened immune function, and an increased risk of heart disease. Cortisol is also known to affect the brain's hippocampus, which is responsible for memory and learning. High levels of cortisol over an extended period can lead to hippocampal shrinkage, impairing cognitive functions and increasing the risk of mental health disorders such as depression and anxiety.

Additionally, the constant state of alertness caused by smartphone notifications can disrupt sleep patterns. The blue light emitted by screens interferes with the production of melatonin, the hormone that regulates sleep. Moreover, the habit of checking phones late at night or first thing in the morning can prevent the mind from winding down or properly waking up, leading to poor sleep quality. Poor sleep, in turn, exacerbates stress and contributes to a vicious cycle that can be difficult to break.

The physical effects of stress also extend to musculoskeletal health. The posture many of us adopt when using smartphones—hunched over, with the neck craned forward—can lead to "text neck" and other forms of strain on the back, shoulders, and neck. Over time, this can result in chronic pain and musculoskeletal disorders. The combination of physical strain and stress-induced tension can further exacerbate discomfort, creating a feedback loop of physical and mental stress.

Beyond the immediate physical and mental health risks, the long-term implications of smartphone-induced stress are concerning. Chronic stress is a significant risk factor for a range of serious health conditions, including stroke, diabetes, and even certain types of cancer. The connection between stress and inflammation is well-established, with chronic stress leading to persistent low-level inflammation in the body, which is a known contributor to many chronic diseases.

Moreover, the impact of stress on the brain's plasticity—the ability to adapt and reorganize itself—can lead to long-term cognitive decline. Stress has been shown to reduce neurogenesis, the process by which new neurons are created in the brain, particularly in the hippocampus. This reduction in neurogenesis can impair memory, learning, and overall cognitive function, increasing the risk of neurodegenerative diseases like Alzheimer's.

Given these significant risks, it's crucial to address the role that smartphones play in our stress levels and take proactive steps to mitigate their impact. One effective strategy is to manage notifications more carefully. By turning off non-essential notifications, setting specific times for checking messages and emails, and using "do not disturb" modes during periods of focused work or relaxation, we can reduce the constant barrage of alerts that contribute to stress.

In addition, creating boundaries around smartphone use can help reduce the overall stress burden. This might involve setting designated phone-free times or areas, such as during meals, before bed, or in certain rooms of the house. Engaging in activities that promote relaxation and mental well-being, such as exercise, meditation, or spending time in nature, can also counteract the effects of stress and improve overall health.

Understanding the neuroscience of stress and the physical health risks associated with smartphone use is the first step toward reclaiming control over our mental and physical well-being. By being mindful of how we interact with our devices and taking deliberate steps to reduce stress, we can protect our brains and bodies from the harmful effects of chronic connectivity and live healthier, more balanced lives.

Smartphones, while incredibly useful, have a profound impact on our emotional regulation and decision-making processes. The constant connectivity and barrage of information that come with smartphone use can overwhelm the brain's capacity to manage emotions effectively, leading to poor emotional control and impulsive decision-making.

At the core of emotional regulation is the prefrontal cortex, the part of the brain responsible for planning, decision-making, and moderating social behavior. This region works in tandem with the amygdala, which processes emotions such as fear, anger, and pleasure. In a balanced system, the prefrontal cortex helps keep the amygdala in check, ensuring that our emotional responses are appropriate to the situation and that we can make thoughtful decisions even in the face of strong emotions.

However, the constant influx of notifications, social media updates, and messages that smartphones provide can disrupt this balance. The frequent interruptions demand immediate attention, triggering the amygdala and creating a sense of urgency that can override the prefrontal cortex's regulatory role. This leads to heightened emotional reactivity, where users may find themselves more prone to anger, anxiety, or impulsivity. For instance, a negative comment on social media might provoke an emotional response that is out of proportion to the actual situation, leading to rash decisions or unnecessary stress.

Moreover, the habit of constantly checking smartphones, especially in emotionally charged situations, can prevent individuals from fully processing their emotions. Instead of taking time to reflect and respond thoughtfully, users may react impulsively, driven by the immediate gratification or emotional release that smartphones can provide. This can weaken the brain's ability to regulate emotions over time, making it harder to manage stress, maintain healthy relationships, and make sound decisions.

The impact of smartphones on emotional regulation extends to decision-making as well. The cognitive overload caused by constant connectivity can impair the brain's executive functions, which are crucial for weighing options, considering long-term consequences, and making informed choices. When the brain is bombarded with information and distractions, it becomes more challenging to engage in deep thinking and deliberate decision-making. This can lead to more superficial, short-term decisions driven by immediate emotional responses rather than rational analysis.

Given the significant impact of smartphones on emotional control and decision-making, it's essential to adopt strategies that help manage and reduce smartphone-induced stress. One of the most effective approaches is to implement digital detoxes—periods of time when you deliberately disconnect from your smartphone and other digital devices. A digital detox allows your brain to rest, reducing cognitive overload and giving your emotional regulatory systems time to recalibrate. This break from constant connectivity can lead to improved mood, better focus, and a greater sense of calm.

Digital detoxes can be as simple as setting aside specific times each day to be phone-free, such as during meals, before bed, or during designated "quiet hours." For a more profound impact, consider taking a full day or weekend without your smartphone, using the time to engage in activities that nurture your mental and emotional well-being, such as reading, spending time in nature, or connecting with loved ones face-to-face.

Mindfulness practices are another powerful tool for managing smartphone-induced stress and improving emotional regulation. Mindfulness involves being fully present in the moment, paying attention to your thoughts, feelings, and physical sensations without judgment. By cultivating mindfulness, you can become more aware of how your smartphone use affects your emotions and decision-making processes. This awareness allows you to pause and reflect before reacting, helping you respond to situations with greater clarity and composure.

Mindfulness can be practiced in many ways, from meditation and deep breathing exercises to mindful walking or even mindful smartphone use. For instance, before reaching for your phone, take a moment to check in with yourself—why are you picking it up? Are you seeking distraction, avoiding an uncomfortable emotion, or responding to a genuine need? By becoming more intentional about when and why you use your smartphone, you can reduce its impact on your emotional state and make more conscious, deliberate decisions.

In addition to mindfulness, it's helpful to create a more structured relationship with your smartphone. Setting boundaries around phone use, such as turning off non-essential notifications, using "do not disturb" modes during focus periods, and keeping your phone out of reach during critical tasks, can prevent your device from overwhelming your cognitive and emotional resources. These practices help protect your mental space, allowing you to engage more fully with the present moment and make decisions that align with your long-term goals and values.

In conclusion, while smartphones are powerful tools, they can also disrupt emotional regulation and decision-making processes if not managed carefully. By adopting strategies such as digital detoxes, mindfulness practices, and setting boundaries around phone use, you can reduce the negative impact of smartphones on your mental and emotional well-being. These practices will not only help you regain control over your emotional responses and decision-making but also enhance your overall quality of life in an increasingly digital world.

CHAPTER 7: SOCIAL MEDIA'S ROLE IN MENTAL HEALTH

Doomscrolling, a term that has gained prominence in recent years, refers to the compulsive habit of continuously scrolling through negative news or social media content, particularly during times of crisis. This behavior, driven by the desire to stay informed, often leads to an overwhelming exposure to distressing information, which can have significant psychological consequences. While staying informed is important, the unrelenting consumption of negative content—especially on social media—can contribute to heightened levels of anxiety, depression, and overall emotional distress.

The concept of doomscrolling is rooted in our brain's natural tendency to pay more attention to negative information, a phenomenon known as negativity bias. This bias evolved as a survival mechanism, helping our ancestors stay alert to potential dangers in their environment. However, in today's digital age, where social media algorithms prioritize content that generates strong emotional reactions, this bias can backfire. Platforms like Twitter, Facebook, and Instagram are designed to keep users engaged by showing them content that elicits a response, often through sensational or emotionally charged news. As a result, users are more likely to encounter and dwell on negative stories, whether it's about global crises, political turmoil, or personal tragedies.

The effects of doomscrolling are compounded by the immersive nature of social media. Unlike traditional news sources, which present information in a finite format (such as a newspaper or TV segment), social media offers an endless stream of content. This infinite scroll feature makes it easy to lose track of time and continue consuming more and more distressing news. The more we scroll, the deeper we sink into a cycle of negativity, where each new piece of bad news reinforces feelings of hopelessness and despair.

The psychological toll of doomscrolling is significant. Research has shown that excessive exposure to negative news can lead to increased levels of anxiety and depression. Constantly reading about disasters, conflicts, and other troubling events can create a sense of helplessness, where individuals feel that the world is out of control and that they are powerless to change it. This feeling of powerlessness is a key driver of anxiety and can exacerbate existing mental health issues.

Moreover, doomscrolling can disrupt sleep patterns, which are closely linked to mental health. Many people engage in this behavior late at night, just before going to bed. The flood of negative information stimulates the brain, making it difficult to relax and fall asleep. Poor sleep quality, in turn, is associated with a range of mental health problems, including increased anxiety, irritability, and a greater risk of developing depression.

The effects of doomscrolling are not limited to emotional distress; they can also impact physical health. Chronic stress, which is often fueled by constant exposure to negative news, can lead to a range of physical ailments, including headaches, digestive problems, and weakened immune function. The combination of psychological and physical stress can create a vicious cycle, where individuals feel increasingly overwhelmed and unable to break free from their negative thought patterns.

Breaking the habit of doomscrolling requires a conscious effort to manage one's media consumption and protect mental well-being. One effective strategy is to set specific times for checking the news and social media, rather than allowing it to become a continuous activity throughout the day. For example, limiting news consumption to a few minutes in the morning and evening can help individuals stay informed without becoming overwhelmed.

Another approach is to curate social media feeds to include more positive or neutral content. This might involve following accounts that share uplifting stories, educational content, or hobbies and interests that bring joy. By actively seeking out content that balances the negativity, users can create a more varied and emotionally healthier online experience.

Mindfulness practices can also help counteract the effects of doomscrolling. Techniques such as meditation, deep breathing, or simply taking a few moments to focus on the present moment can help reduce anxiety and bring a sense of calm. These practices can also increase self-awareness, making it easier to recognize when doomscrolling is starting to take a toll and to take steps to stop it.

Finally, digital detoxes—periods of time where individuals disconnect from social media and news altogether—can be incredibly beneficial. Whether it's for a few hours, a day, or even longer, taking a break from the constant flow of information allows the mind to reset and recover from the stress of continuous negative exposure.

In conclusion, while staying informed is important, it's crucial to recognize the psychological risks of doomscrolling. By understanding how social media contributes to anxiety and depression, and by taking proactive steps to manage media consumption, individuals can protect their mental health and maintain a more balanced and positive outlook on the world.

In the era of personalized content, social media platforms have become powerful tools for connecting people, sharing information, and fostering communities. However, these same platforms also pose significant risks, particularly through the creation of echo chambers and the spread of misinformation. The algorithms that drive social media are designed to maximize user engagement by showing content that aligns with users' interests and beliefs. While this can create a more tailored online experience, it also has the unintended consequence of reinforcing biases and isolating users from diverse perspectives.

Echo chambers occur when social media algorithms repeatedly expose users to content that confirms their existing beliefs, while filtering out content that challenges or contradicts those views. Over time, this can create a distorted sense of reality, where users believe that their perspective is the only valid one, simply because it is the one they encounter most frequently. This reinforcement of biases can lead to polarization, where individuals become more entrenched in their views and less open to alternative opinions.

The danger of echo chambers is compounded by the spread of misinformation. Social media algorithms prioritize content that generates strong emotional reactions—whether it's anger, fear, or excitement—because such content is more likely to be shared and commented on, thus driving more engagement. Unfortunately, misinformation and sensationalized content often provoke these

reactions, making them more likely to go viral. When users are consistently exposed to misleading or false information within their echo chambers, they may come to accept it as truth, further entrenching their biases and contributing to a divided and misinformed society.

The spread of misinformation is not just a theoretical concern; it has real-world consequences. During elections, public health crises, and other critical events, the proliferation of false information can influence public opinion, sway political outcomes, and even endanger lives. For example, during the COVID-19 pandemic, misinformation about the virus and vaccines spread rapidly on social media, leading to confusion, fear, and in some cases, resistance to public health measures. The echo chamber effect exacerbated this issue, as users who were already skeptical of vaccines were more likely to encounter and believe anti-vaccine propaganda, further solidifying their stance.

Given these challenges, it is crucial to find ways to responsibly engage with social media to minimize its negative impacts while still benefiting from its positive aspects. One of the most effective strategies for breaking out of echo chambers is to actively seek out diverse perspectives. This can be done by following a variety of accounts that represent different viewpoints, engaging with content from across the political and ideological spectrum, and being open to challenging one's own beliefs. By exposing oneself to a wider range of opinions, users can develop a more nuanced understanding of complex issues and reduce the risk of becoming trapped in an echo chamber.

Critical thinking is another essential tool for navigating social media responsibly. Before accepting or sharing information, it's important to evaluate the credibility of the source, check for supporting evidence, and consider whether the content might be designed to provoke an emotional reaction rather than inform. Fact-checking websites and tools can be invaluable in this process, helping users to verify the accuracy of information before passing it along.

Limiting exposure to emotionally charged content can also help reduce the impact of misinformation and echo chambers. Social media platforms often amplify content that evokes strong emotions, but these emotions can cloud judgment and lead to impulsive reactions. By taking a step back and reflecting before engaging with such content, users can avoid being swept up in the emotional wave and make more thoughtful decisions about what to believe and share.

Balancing social media use also involves setting boundaries around time spent on these platforms. Excessive social media use has been linked to negative mental health outcomes, including increased anxiety, depression, and feelings of isolation. To mitigate these effects, it's helpful to establish specific times of day for checking social media, rather than allowing it to become a constant presence. Taking regular breaks from social media, such as during meals, before bed, or on weekends, can also help reduce its hold on one's attention and mental state.

In addition to setting time boundaries, it's beneficial to engage in activities that provide a counterbalance to the often overwhelming nature of social media. Spending time in nature, practicing mindfulness or meditation, reading books, or engaging in face-to-face conversations can all help ground individuals in reality and foster a sense of connection and well-being that social media alone cannot provide.

Finally, it's important to remember that social media algorithms are not neutral; they are designed to maximize engagement, often at the expense of accuracy and diversity. By being aware of how these algorithms work and making conscious choices about how to interact with social media, users can take control of their online experience rather than being passively shaped by it.

In conclusion, while social media has the potential to connect us and enhance our lives, it also poses significant risks through the creation of echo chambers and the spread of misinformation. By actively seeking out diverse perspectives, practicing critical thinking, setting boundaries, and engaging in balancing activities, individuals can responsibly navigate the social media landscape, minimizing its negative impacts and making the most of its benefits.

CHAPTER 8: THE PATH FORWARD - RECLAIMING YOUR MIND

In an age where smartphones dominate our daily routines, the idea of a digital detox—reducing or even eliminating smartphone use—can seem daunting, yet many individuals have taken this step and experienced profound positive changes in their lives. These success stories offer inspiring examples of how taking control of technology use can lead to improved well-being, deeper relationships, and greater mental clarity.

One such story comes from Sarah, a marketing professional who found herself constantly tethered to her phone. Sarah realized that her smartphone was consuming an increasing amount of her time and energy, often leaving her feeling overwhelmed and stressed. She decided to embark on a digital detox, starting with small steps like turning off notifications and setting specific times to check her phone. Over time, she extended her detox to include phone-free weekends and social media breaks. The result? Sarah noticed a significant reduction in her stress levels, improved focus at work, and more meaningful interactions with her friends and family. She found that by disconnecting from her phone, she was able to reconnect with the things that truly mattered in her life.

Another success story is that of John, a writer who struggled with smartphone addiction. John realized that his constant scrolling through social media and news apps was not only eating into his productivity but also affecting his mental health. Determined to regain control, he decided to take a more drastic approach: he switched to a basic, non-smartphone for several months. During this time, John rediscovered the joy of reading, writing, and engaging in hobbies he had long neglected. Without the constant pull of his smartphone, he found that he was able to think more deeply, sleep better, and feel more present in his daily life. Although he eventually returned to using a smartphone, John now uses it with a heightened awareness and has maintained many of the boundaries he established during his detox.

Then there's Emily, a teacher who noticed that her smartphone was affecting her relationships with her students and colleagues. She often found herself distracted during conversations, checking her phone during meetings, and feeling disconnected from those around her. Emily decided to implement a digital detox focused on mindfulness. She began by leaving her phone in her bag during work hours and committing to being fully present in her interactions. This small change had a ripple effect—Emily became more engaged with her students, more attentive in meetings, and even noticed improvements in her own mental health. She felt less anxious, more focused, and more in tune with her environment.

These stories highlight the transformative power of reducing smartphone dependence, and they offer practical insights into how you can begin your own digital detox journey. Here are some practical tips to help you start making changes in your daily life:

1. **Start Small and Gradually Increase**: You don't have to eliminate smartphone use all at once. Begin with small changes, like turning off non-essential notifications or setting specific times to check your phone. As you become more comfortable, you can extend these periods and explore more significant steps like phone-free mornings or weekends.

2. **Set Clear Boundaries**: Create physical and temporal boundaries for smartphone use. Designate specific areas of your home, such as the bedroom or dining room, as phone-free zones. Similarly, establish times of day when you will not use your phone, such as during meals, before bed, or when spending time with loved ones.

3. **Use Tools to Help You Disconnect**: Many smartphones now offer digital wellbeing features that can help you monitor and manage your usage. Set daily screen time limits, use "do not disturb" modes during focus periods, or try apps designed to block distracting sites and notifications during designated times.

4. **Replace Phone Time with Meaningful Activities**: Identify activities that you enjoy and that do not involve screens, such as reading, exercising, cooking, or spending time outdoors. By filling your day with these activities, you'll find it easier to resist the urge to check your phone.

5. **Practice Mindfulness**: Incorporate mindfulness practices into your daily routine to increase your awareness of how and why you use your smartphone. Before picking up your phone, take a moment to reflect on whether you genuinely need to use it or if you're seeking distraction. Mindful use of technology can help you break the habit of mindless scrolling and

make more intentional choices about your phone use.

6. **Connect with Others in Real Life**: Make an effort to prioritize face-to-face interactions over digital communication. Arrange in-person meetings with friends and family, and focus on being fully present during these interactions. Strengthening real-world connections can reduce the need to rely on your smartphone for social fulfillment.

7. **Try a Digital Detox Challenge**: Consider committing to a short-term digital detox challenge, such as going a full day or weekend without your smartphone. These challenges can help you reset your relationship with technology and gain a fresh perspective on how you want to use your devices moving forward.

8. **Reflect on Your Experience**: After making changes to your smartphone use, take time to reflect on the effects. Do you feel less stressed? More focused? Happier? Use these reflections to

motivate yourself to continue making positive changes and to adjust your approach as needed.

A digital detox doesn't mean giving up your smartphone entirely; rather, it's about finding a balance that allows you to enjoy the benefits of technology without sacrificing your mental and emotional well-being. By following these tips and learning from the experiences of others, you can begin to reclaim control over your smartphone use and experience the positive changes that come with a more mindful, intentional relationship with technology.

In today's fast-paced, technology-driven world, it's easy to fall into the habit of spending countless hours on our smartphones, often without even realizing it. While these devices offer incredible convenience and connectivity, they can also detract from activities that truly enrich our lives. Building healthy habits that encourage the replacement of smartphone time with more fulfilling pursuits is not just beneficial for our well-being—it's essential for leading a balanced and meaningful life.

One of the most powerful ways to counteract excessive smartphone use is by incorporating regular physical exercise into your routine. Exercise not only benefits your physical health but also boosts mental clarity, reduces stress, and improves overall mood. Whether it's a brisk walk in the park, a yoga session, or a workout at the gym, physical activity provides a natural break from screens and allows you to reconnect with your body and surroundings. The time spent moving your body can serve as a refreshing reset, helping you return to your tasks with renewed focus and energy.

Reading physical books is another enriching activity that can effectively replace time spent on smartphones. Unlike the fragmented and often superficial experience of reading on a screen, diving into a physical book encourages deep, focused engagement with the material. The tactile experience of holding a book, the absence of digital distractions, and the linear progression of turning pages all contribute to a more immersive and satisfying reading experience. Whether it's fiction, non-fiction, or even poetry, reading allows you to expand your mind, explore new ideas, and develop a richer understanding of the world.

Engaging in face-to-face conversations is yet another valuable habit that can greatly enhance your life. While digital communication has its place, nothing compares to the depth and connection that comes from interacting with others in person. Face-to-face conversations allow for the full range of human expression—tone of voice, body language, eye contact—all of which contribute to a more meaningful and authentic exchange. These interactions strengthen relationships, build empathy, and create lasting memories that can't be replicated through a screen.

In addition to these activities, exploring hobbies and interests that don't involve screens can also help create a healthier balance. Whether it's gardening, cooking, painting, playing a musical instrument, or volunteering, engaging in hands-on, creative activities provides a sense of fulfillment and accomplishment that is often missing from the instant gratification of smartphone use. These hobbies not only occupy your time in a productive and enjoyable way but also help you develop new skills and passions that can enrich your life for years to come.

As we look ahead, it's clear that the choices we make today about how we use technology will have lasting implications for future generations and society as a whole. Conscious technology use is not just about reducing screen time—it's about fostering a healthier relationship with technology that enhances our lives rather than detracts from it.

For future generations, the habits we model and the values we instill will shape their relationship with technology. By prioritizing real-world experiences, meaningful interactions, and personal growth over digital consumption, we can teach children and young adults the importance of balance. Encouraging them to explore the world beyond screens, to develop hobbies, and to build strong interpersonal relationships will equip them with the tools they need to navigate the digital age with resilience and wisdom.

On a broader societal level, conscious technology use is crucial for maintaining our collective well-being. As technology continues to evolve, it is essential that we remain mindful of its impact on our mental health, social connections, and cognitive abilities. By adopting a more intentional approach to technology, we can mitigate the negative effects of excessive screen time, such as decreased attention spans, increased stress, and social isolation. Instead, we can harness the power of technology to connect, create, and contribute to a better world.

The future of technology is undoubtedly exciting, with innovations that have the potential to improve our lives in countless ways. However, it is up to us to ensure that these advancements serve our highest interests and do not come at the cost of our humanity. By building healthy habits, prioritizing enriching activities, and encouraging conscious technology use, we can create a future where technology enhances our lives without diminishing the things that make us truly human.

As you move forward, consider the habits you want to cultivate and the impact you want to have on those around you. By making small, intentional changes in how you use technology, you can reclaim your time, enrich your life, and set a positive example for others. The journey to a healthier, more balanced relationship with technology begins with the choices you make today—choices that will shape not only your future but the future of generations to come.

CONCLUSION

As we reach the conclusion of this exploration into the impact of smartphones on our lives, it's clear that these devices, while powerful and indispensable tools, carry significant implications for our cognitive function, emotional well-being, and overall quality of life. Throughout this book, we have delved into various aspects of smartphone use, from the neuroscience of stress to the dangers of echo chambers, and from the erosion of our memory muscle to the addictive behaviors that these devices can foster.

We began by examining the historical context and rapid evolution of smartphones, which have seamlessly integrated into every aspect of our lives. We explored how these devices exploit our brain's dopamine system, creating feedback loops that keep us hooked and engaged often to our detriment. We also looked at the cognitive toll that smartphones take, including the reduction in hippocampus size and gray matter, and how this translates into everyday challenges such as dependency on GPS and forgetfulness.

The psychological impacts of smartphone addiction were another critical area of focus. We discussed how constant connectivity and notifications can lead to increased anxiety, withdrawal symptoms, and a decrease in our attention spans. Furthermore, we explored the concept of brain drain, where even the mere presence of a smartphone can reduce our cognitive performance, and how this affects our ability to engage in deep thinking and make informed decisions.

We also highlighted the role of social media in contributing to anxiety and depression through practices like doomscrolling, and how algorithm-driven content can create echo chambers that reinforce biases and isolate us from diverse perspectives. In response to these challenges, we outlined practical strategies for reducing smartphone dependence, such as digital detoxes, mindfulness practices, and building healthy habits that prioritize more enriching activities like exercise, reading, and face-to-face interactions.

As we reflect on the broader implications of smartphone overuse, it becomes evident that this issue extends beyond individual well-being. The way we engage with technology shapes our society, influences our relationships, and impacts the mental health of future generations. If left unchecked, the pervasive influence of smartphones could lead to a more disconnected, distracted, and mentally fatigued society.

However, this future is not inevitable. The power to change lies in our hands, quite literally. By taking proactive steps to manage our smartphone use, we can reclaim our cognitive abilities, strengthen our emotional resilience, and foster deeper, more meaningful connections with the world around us. The benefits of these changes are profound—improved focus, reduced stress, enhanced memory, and a greater sense of balance and fulfillment in our lives.

The call to action is clear: it's time to reassess our relationship with technology and take control of how we interact with it. Start by implementing small changes, like setting boundaries for phone use, engaging in digital detoxes, and replacing screen time with activities that nourish your mind and body. Be mindful of how your smartphone habits affect your mental health and well-being, and make conscious choices that align with your values and long-term goals.

As you move forward, remember that the journey to healthier smartphone use is a gradual process, and every step you take towards greater balance is a step towards a healthier, more fulfilling life. By embracing conscious technology use, not only do you improve your own well-being, but you also contribute to a society that values mindfulness, connection, and genuine human interaction.

The future is in your hands—literally and figuratively. Choose wisely, live mindfully, and take control of your digital life for a healthier mind, a richer life, and a more connected world.

www.ingramcontent.com/pod-product-compliance
Lightning Source LLC
LaVergne TN
LVHW051714050326
832903LV00032B/4204